D1194758

Dorothy Molloy
Long-distance Swimmer

salmonpoetry

Published in 2009 by
Salmon Poetry
Cliffs of Moher, County Clare, Ireland
Website: www.salmonpoetry.com
Email: info@salmonpoetry.com

ISBN 978-1-907056-21-5

Cover artwork: *Carrie Herries* (www.hallocards.co.uk)
Cover design & typesetting: *Siobhán Hutson*
Printed in England by imprint*digital*.net

Acknowledgements

Two of these poems have been published previously: 'Waiting for Julio', which won third prize in the Féile Filíochta International Poetry Competition in 2000, was published in the pamphlet containing the prize-winning poems and on the internet by Dun Laoghaire-Rathdown County Council. 'November Visit' was published, under a slightly different title, in *The SHOp*, summer 2003.

Contents

Preface

When Dorothy Molloy died of cancer on 4 January 2004, just ten days before the publication of her first collection, *Hare Soup*, Ireland lost a distinctive poetic voice. Soon after her death, I realised that her papers contained many poems that were either complete or nearly complete. From this material, I have been able to assemble two posthumous collections of her poetry, *Gethsemane Day* which was published by Faber and Faber in 2006, and the current collection, *Long-distance Swimmer*.

Long-distance Swimmer is a strange and moving book inspired by the experiences of Dorothy's life in Spain and Ireland and also by her wide reading and her need to explore, for herself and others, the mysteries of connections and separations, the paradoxes of life and love. It contains some remarkable and passionate poems that deserve a wide readership.

Now, nearly six years after Dorothy's death, it is good to know that more and more critics are paying attention to her work. I look forward to the first book on her poetry, being written by Dr Luz Mar Gonzáles Arias of the University of Oviedo, which will set her work into a European as well as an Irish context.

Among those who have been instrumental in helping bring this book to publication are Jonathan Williams, Lucy Collins, Luz Mar Gonzáles Arias, the members of the Thornfield Poets, Éilís Ní Dhuibhne, and Gerry Lyne and the staff in the Manuscripts Section of the National Library of Ireland (where Dorothy's papers are now housed). Dorothy would have been delighted to know that Salmon was publishing her work, and we all owe Jessie Lendennie, Siobhán Hutson and the team many thanks for producing this final collection so beautifully.

ANDREW CARPENTER
Dublin, August 2009

Mother's kitchen

Mother's kitchen – it's laid out
on the terrazzo floor;
marble galaxies beneath her feet,

dead wasps in the jam-jar;
the Aga throbs with heat.
And Maggie,

           her bag
full of stolen trinkets, humdy-dumdies
down the stairs, her hair sticking out,

out like a bottle-brush,
her sister still threatening

to throw herself off
the end of
the pier.

Death by drowning

You pin your hair up in a bun,
step out of your skirt, dive in.
The sea shivers round your waist
like a petticoat of silk.

You swim past pretty cottages
and rows of boats fragmenting
in the waves. Outside the harbour
the undertow twirls you about.

You turn on your back; head
for the island through buffet and toss.
Cross-currents tear at your grips,
pull down your hair. Blinded,

you kick at the sea. Arms windmill and
grope. Water spills into your
mouth, sandbags you down
through piston-rod, hammer and pound.

For an instant, the heap of your hair
floats like a raft on the spot
where the sea sucks you in. Half-daft,
too late to beg pardon,

we wait for your wreckage to land.
We harden our grief into rituals,
requiems, wreaths. You drift back
in your own sweet time.

Going your own way

You swim out in your underwear,
your skirt discarded
on the harbour wall.

You don a mantilla of spume,
the rope of your hair trailing
like kelp in your wake.

You head for the Kish. Its bright eye
blinking a way forward
like a sanctuary lamp.

You crawl over seas of granite.
Flurries of foam pull
at your petrified ankles.

You hear water-bells clang;
clappers of iron and salt
salute you *en passant*.

You lean on waves of cold
comfort before
going

                        down

Fledgling

Cooped up in a birdcage at eighty,
she pecks on a cuttlefish bone,
decks out her new home: silver bells,
ladders and swings.

In mirrors that dangle like moons
from the sky, she finds look-alike friends:
discreet parakeets with scimitar
beaks like her own.

But they're dumb. She tempts them with rum
from Jamaica, with sips of the sweetest
Jerez, with truffles and chocolates,
with pink gin and cakes.

She gives them a peek at her treasures,
gold sovereigns, carbuncles and rings;
the knick-knacks he gave her, the way
he enslaved her, the rubies

he slung round her neck. What the heck.
She kohls her frail eyelids, blushes
her cheeks, hangs upside-down
on her perch. She ruffles

her feathers, she whistles and sings;
she feels the first stretch

of her wings.

Chez moi

I'm only at home on the hill now,
walking my dog among trees,
or curled out the back with my cat.

People – I take them or leave them;
it's all touch and go, except
for the man in the deer-stalker hat

who pops up now and then in my bed.
Shadowy children flit round
in the wings. I used to be yearning

but now I've no time for such things.
I light scented candles. I stand
on my head. I make no more scenes.

Parents die off or wear thin, but drag on.
Siblings of sixty and more
are bickering still. It's a scream.

We're all too far gone. I've named
my executor, drawn up my will;
I can feel my hide thicken. Inside

there's new skin. I can't hang around people
for ever, I've got things to do
on the moon. Trees leave me alone,

don't ask questions, are there;
candelabra of seasons in bud,
fairy lights that switch on in the gorse.

There's a door in the rock
at a place where the salt sea flows
into the sky; I can squeeze through
to Wales.

The see-saw

Lurching on the see-saw of marriage,
the hard plank under your bottom,
you gasp at the repeated jolts
that shiver your timbers.

You grasp at straws, your wedding dress
coming away in your hands.
Your teeth are bared,
your eyes squeezed tight.
You are losing your
balance.
The black mop of your hair
flops over your face,
and your veil is wild
around your ears.

The third finger of your left hand
is branded with a ring.
As the lurching continues,
you struggle to pull your skirt
down over your knees.
One of your shoes has fallen
into the mud.

Your mother can't help you now.
She sits at right angles to you,
heavy in her apron, staring
at her lap.

A little girl stands with her back
to the wall, sucking her thumb.
She waits for her turn. She has a butterfly
bow in her hair and white wedding
shoes on her feet.

Forbidden fruit

1

He loved dark chocolate, speckled melons, quince.
With fingers that were trembling, touched the ripening
fruits. His mother had to hide the sweet
preserves. He rooted round the attic til
he found the deep glass jars, and speared with knitting
needles woozy cherries, apricots
and peaches, drunken blue-black grapes.

A prince among his siblings (his mother said
that he could sing before he learnt to speak),
his parents, forty cousins, uncles, aunts,
the cooks and maids, the workers on the land,
all jumped at his command. They knew that
Federico, from the moment of his birth,
could hear the bells that ring beneath the earth.

A phosphorescent child (since lightning left its
kiss upon his cheek) he walked along
the river-paths, half-dazed among the willows
and the hollyhocks, wild celery and yellow-flowered
fennel, umbelliferous. He built an altar
on the garden wall, said Mass in mother's
frock; but when a troupe of puppeteers

arrived in town, he could not eat or sleep until
he'd torn the altar down, set up a little
theatre instead. He begged his old
wet-nurse to fashion rag and cardboard dolls.
And then he started on his puppet-plays.

2

In formal suit and white starched shirt and patent leather
shoes, he set out for the 'Resi'
in Madrid, his hair combed back to show his widow's
peak. Unspeakable the things he felt for
Salvador, Emilio. Their merest glances
left him flushed and weak.

3

Terrified of sex and sin, the swelling purple
aubergine, he crossed the ocean, paced Manhattan
streets. If only he could be a child
again and fall asleep on Cobos Rueda's
knee, and talk to plants and listen
to the stars. In waking dreams his favourite cousins
loomed: Aurelia (the one who hated

thunderstorms), Matilda and Clothilde.
The irrigation streams, the *regadío*,
kept flowing in his brain. Insane the winter
smell of pent-up water that came from every
house, the ghostly glow of oil-lamps newly
lit, the half-scorched wings of moths.
He used to be a *monaguillo* once,

an altar-boy, the Baby Jesus blessing him
with fingerless white hands. But now male lovers
beckoned him. He posed, Christ-like, against a tree,
his arms stretched out. And then succumbed. Delirious,
half-numbed, he wrote of nightingales and daggers;
of lemons, blood-red poppies, seedless fruits.

4

A lecture tour in Cuba set him free.
He swam with naked blackmen in the sea.

The sky was Málaga-blue and oh, the heat;
the endless beat of bongo-drums, the slow sad
habaneras, the rattle of a thousand beads
in hollow dried-out gourds. Drunk on the scent
of orchids and magnolias, and heady draughts of

sticky sugar-cane, he lost count of the
one-night stands, drew sustenance, they say,
from rum and cups of coffee, *chambola de
guanábaná* and pungent fat cigars.
Stretched on his bed in Hotel La Unión,
he read his poems to dozens of young men
and breakfasted on honey-bread at noon.

5

After a season in the Cuban sun,
Federico yearned again for Algeciras,
Cádiz, Alcalá de los Gazules,
and burned a trail for Spain. Granada was still
there; the Alpujarras, Cáñar,
La Calahorra and Guadix; the washerwomen
singing as before, the shepherds

with grave faces tending sheep, la Casa
del Zagal. The Virgin of Good Love
in her tin crown lit up her spangles, and Federico,
laughing, struck the window-bars of home
with a small metallic spoon and played
a wild carillon to the moon.

6

In August nineteen thirty-six, the death-squad came.
They trampled down the jasmine and the bright blooms
of the pomegranate bushes; primed their rifles,
roaring out his name.

One Easter

One Easter you left me there
to walk the dry hills alone,
flies nesting in my hair,
the sun burning a hole
in my nape.

I walked past mountainy cows
with wooden bells and tongue-tied
Spanish shepherds tending
their sheep.

Up on the peak the Snow Virgin
did as she was bid. She heard your prayer.
She was there when the waterfall
leapt to its death; and was swept over
the black rocks below in a ragged white
drift.

She was there when I navigated
the swish-car roads, the hairpin bends,
the merry-go-round loops of the path
that led to your door. She was there
when your mother leaned out over the balcony
to sooth her tattered nerves
with the sound of water sucked
into hollow spaces, swirling like
a mad whippers in the gorges,
waiting in the drowning-holes
for such as I,

left to walk the dry hills alone,
the flies nesting in my hair,
the sun burning a hole
in my nape. I wrapped my cardigan
round my head like a scarf
and reached, as I said, your mother's door.

She stared at me. Mute.
So I sang her a song in my own tongue.
Told her how far I had come
and how cruel was her son
who had cruelly left her
and me to walk the dry hills
alone.

She sat in a kitchen chair,
hands folded on her lap. We cried
and listened to the water suck. After,
she made me an omelette,
gave me some cooked ham still
wrapped in a bag, and rubbed ripe
tomatoes into a loaf of bread.
We ate. Drank the weak table wine.
Pale pink with a flush of sugar-water.
She called me her daughter.

Next morning, I picked myself up,
dragged myself to the station. Lost sight
of the Snow Virgin when the train swept me
away. Sparks jumped off the tracks when
we reached the next valley. But I did not
give up my devotion to her. Spurred on
by the fact that you left me to walk

the dry hills by myself. Till I found
your mother wandering there too.
We protected each other from the flies.
From the heat of the sun.

Christmas in the Pyrenees

Smells of hot chocolate and snow drift into the room.
With fingers on fire, I rush to the frozen pane.
I melt a peep-hole and look: the mountains rise sheer
like fat wax candles pressing against the sky.

Your mother is setting the table; she pokes at the stove.
She looks up at you with the usual sobs in her eyes.
Your stepfather rustles the paper; he works at his sums
with the butt of a pencil, moving his lips as he tots.

Cheap chandeliers hang low over our heads.
Your mother brings in the cups, lays her hand on your arm.
She sits in her chair, then straightens her apron and sighs.
The river flows down the ravine and past the back door.

It's Christmas and Jesus is laid on his bed of fake fur.
A halo held firm with two nails at the back of his neck.
His plaster legs beat at the air, his hands clasp in prayer.
His vitreous eyes, dark as hers, catching mine, catching yours.

Down in the village the Wise Men appear on a cart:
Balthazar, Melchior, Caspar, one daubed with soot.
Startling in scarlet and gold, their crowns at a tilt,
they trundle ahead of the crowd, throwing out sweets.

The small mountain ponies are panting, they strain at the slope;
steam swirls from their nostrils, sparks fly from their
    clattering hooves.
They come to a halt at the church; Mass-bells echo on rock
as we rise from the table in silence and glance at the clock.

Carlitos González Martínez makes a desperate bid for freedom

His three-year-old face was an ivory moon.
He never got out:
the overweight toddler from Tamarit Street,
puffing great baby with infantile feet;
I led him away to the sea.

His three-year-old face was yoghurt and milk.
His little heart beat
like a drum in my fist when he took his first steps
from Tamarit Street. Not a minute too soon
I led him away to the sea.

I showed him the birds on the Ramblas, in cages,
the budgies and cockatoos,
parrots, canaries; the bare-bottomed monkeys
on silver-chain leashes, that screeched as Carlitos
passed by on his way to the sea.

We went to the market, bought apricots, peaches,
black olives and anchovies,
almonds and quinces; *chorizos*, *serranos*,
manchegos and *churros* to keep up our strength
as we came within sight of the sea.

We boarded the three-masted *Santa María*,
we chugged round the port
on the white *golondrina*. We sat on the beach
at the Barceloneta where oysters and octopus
dance in the diamond-bright sea.

We took the quick lift up Columbus's monument.
Paid a peseta
to peep through the telescope, scan the horizon

for new worlds and islands, Mallorca, Menorca,
not Tamarit Street where they never

heard tell of the sea. I went down by the stairs.
'But not I', cried Carlitos
González Martínez. An outgrown *putto*
with pink pudgy wings, he took to the air.
His three-year-old face a lit candle,

a rose, he waved *adiós* to Tamarit
Street and said 'Hello sea'
to the sea.

Gypsy dancer in the caves at Sacromonte

At first his castanets produced a fluttering,
a kind of small talk, *sotto voce* stuff.

And then there was a flurry in the brown cups
of his hands: a sound of birds all twittering

and bickering and cracking nuts. Trapped between
his palms, he held them on the very edge

of flight. With slow tap-tapping toes,
he moved along the full length of the cave

to where I stood, and there he stopped. I gulped the wine.
Suddenly,

his hands commotioning behind his back,
he teetered on his heels, his ankles

undulating, if you please, as though they'd turned
to butter, like my knees.

Waiting for Julio

Maria nearly died

when Julio came upon her, feeding slops to the pigs.
But it was love at first sight.

He made friends with her father, put a ring on her finger
and gave her a son.

In his letters from the Front, he called her 'My Jewel';
sent kisses to the boy.

While the Civil War raged, she slept on one half
of the bed, molly-coddled

the baby, kept Julio's pillows plumped up,
embroidered his name

in the linen, and busied herself with the sheets.
She soaked them in troughs

of dark water behind the house. She scrubbed them
on washboards of stone.

She dragged them up steps to the kitchen, in buckets
and basins and tubs.

She strung them out neat on a line that stretched taut
from her window to peaks

that poked holes in the sky. She pegged them on tight.
Clouds of carbolic

hung over the house and got under her skin.
All the other men died

in the war, or came back to the village, but Julio
hovered betwixt.

He appeared one day with a rug round his shoulders,
his eyes out on sticks.

He pushed past 'My Jewel', the baby, the bed,
and curled up in the cot;

plugging his ears with his whimpering hands,
he made soft sucking sounds

with his lips.

Back patio

Under the giant palm tree
behind the patio wall,
I suffer when I see the clay:
the place where tom cats shit
and slugs lay slime, and fronds
fall dead.

I stand on all four feet
and lock my joints. Project
my fur-balls onto broccoli
and honeysuckle, pink
and blue hydrangea.

The lily-cups sit on the water-table:
purple, pink and white.
The lily pads are green and flat.
Like plates.

I shoulder my three cats,
quick stroke and purr.
Inject the insulin.
Then back to work.
I clear away the excrement,
clean out the litter-tray,
the heaps of heavy sand,
dark perfume of testosterone,
the steroid-treated male.

Geraniums grow red and violent
in their tubs. Tomato vines
hang sweet. Sweet peas climb up
the bamboo pole and loop the loop.

Behind the giant palm
the tap is dripping.
The hose writhes like a snake.
It spits at spiders, lunges at the ants and aphids,
spouts at water-mint. It lashes
at the grey stone slabs, uproots
the tiny strawberries,
self-seeded in the gap.

Quadruped with my quadrupeds

Quadruped with my quadrupeds
I crawl. Cats under the arch
of my belly, tails erect, touch
the goddess of their plenty.

Yawning on summer walls
or stretching on the gravel,
I examine my claws, retracting
my nails when you pet me.

In my basket of cushions I wait
for your hand. Your fingerprints
carry my code. I embed
myself in the whorls
of your flesh.

All day, heavy as stone,
I rest on dark weaves
of desire, waiting
for you to come home.

Then you lift me, warm,
onto your shoulder,
and carry me down
to the shiny white door.

I tighten my claws
on your nape, nip
at your ear.

You prise me off gently,
unfurl me in the long grass.

Soon we are out of sight:
she-cat in season, howling,
receiving her mate.

Peregrino

Three sets of hands are upon him
as the needle probes for the vein
and plunges the purple of death
into the pain.

Rent with his cry, I stroke
the blind fur. 'It's alright', I lie.
He sinks on soft knees, falls
in a tangle of paws.

The nurse straightens his limbs,
lays him out on his side; his heart
like a bird in the dark flutter
of stethoscope.

Propped against walls that keep edging
away, I catch sight of his wide-open
eyes. His pupils dilate.
They wax like the moon,

fill the room
with a nocturnal
light.

Dog–kite

I used to hold her
by a silver chain
that linked us
like a vein.

Now she's a comet,
dammit,
all wag-tail
and bright eye.

I see her whizz
between the stars;
she flares and disappears
in the night sky.

She left her paw-marks
in the wet cement.

My fireworks, the stars

My fireworks, the stars
exploding over my head
tonight, whizzing around
clouds, regrouping in
dense clusters, scattering
again, fading, falling,
shooting, hiding behind the
chimneys, nesting in trees,
and resting, finally, in the glass
wells of my binoculars.

The stars explode over my
head. Dogs bark as they
crackle, sizzle, fizz and pop
across the sky. The three cats
leap into my lap, eyes big as
saucers, ears pointing backwards.
Claws hook, tails twitch.

My stars flare like matches
unsteady as sulphur flame
in the quiet nothingness of the
sky. I reach up and pick them
one by one like silver daisies
out of the black field over my head.
They glow and tinkle like bells.
They are quite prickly.
They burn as I string them round my neck.

At Winchester

We spend the night in the cathedral,
cool our fevered bodies
on the stone.

Stretched out along the full length
of the nave, ear to the ground,
we hear

the drowning waters lapping
in the crypt. Ravished angels
rhapsody

behind the screen. Somewhere between
the gargoyles and the carven
miserichords,

recumbent figures sleep
as if they're dead. At break of day
we rise up

from our marble bed. Renew
our marriage vow. May Emily
and Swithin

help us now.

In December it's dark

In December it's dark
in Lapland.
You travel by sleigh
along snow-paths,
your way lit up by
bonfires, while shadows
play among the fir trees,
each with a star at its
tip.

In Russia, the horses
neigh as they pull the
troikas up and down the
towns and race the trains
from Moscow to St. Petersburg.
And they snort and steam
and tinkle their bells
and the ice crackles
and the hackles of
wild dogs rise in the
steppe and Rasputin
cackles and sips his
cyanide, while the
skirts of the Romanov
girls whirl and swirl
like snowflakes, and
they huddle to keep
warm and they cuddle
Alexei, the prince with the
sailor hat. And their hands
freeze, and they wheeze
as the surprise bullets
go through them.

Tinderbox

Wild boars blink in the sun. Bolt.
The deer merge with the trees. Birds
fly away between dawn and dusk. Black
spiders dangle and weave. Bunnies
burrow deep. Hornets buzz
between us as we bend
our heads over the map. Blink.
We have lost our bearings
in this atrium of leaf, branch,
twig and trunk.

We cannot find the star-blaze
where the six paths meet. Behold,
I send you forth with your beloved
son. Blinded,
I wait till you disappear over the brink.

The forest catches its breath.
Blanches,
when I open the box.
Strike a match. Blow
it out.

Sister Death

Sister Death walks in through the door of my head
jangling her keys, while I'm still in bed.
I say, 'You can stay now. Sit down. Bide your time.
You belong to me fully now. Finally. Mine.'

I wanted to keep you out there in the cold,
to keep you locked out even as I grew old.
I thought if I managed to keep that door shut,
I'd escape death myself, live a deathless life, but

a shadow grew up that attacked me instead,
wrapped me round like a shroud, came to live in my head;
like a dangerous madwoman locked in a cell,
she rattled her shackles and gave me pure hell.

Now that Death has come in and I've got her name,
that Shadow's gone out, and I'm not the same;
no longer resisting, I open my head
to my own Sister Death lying with me, in bed

so close to my body, wherever I go,
till finally, one day, we'll both go below;
but this morning I waken to bird cries and blue,
to frost and fogged windows, and life that is new.

I'm listening to Stabat Mater

I'm listening to Stabat Mater.
The choirs pass by like ships
in full sail under the
cliff of dream. 'To thine
own self be true,' a voice rings
out, piercing me like a
needle. The cats are in
bed. The dog waits for his
supper. The clock whirrs
round on invisible springs,
and the moon hides behind
blackberry clouds, its face
all sticky and smeared.
The veils of the temple are torn.

When mother comes, she will
re-set the pendulums of
hope. I hear words like
'desolate' and see people standing
at the foot of their own
crucifixes or impaled
thereon. Each to his own.
Her own.

I'm listening to Stabat Mater.
The choirs pass by like ships
in full sail, under the
cliff of dream.

I wake up in quicksand

I wake up in quicksand,
hear the heavy feet of night
retreating behind slammed
doors. The day is waiting
to be reinvented. The heavy clay
shapeless on the table of
morning. Dogs are whimpering in the
corners of my mind and desperate
children refuse to go to school.

The nuns come, swaggering, in big
black tents, swinging their monster
beads. The clocks have stopped
ticking. In the silence, I fill my
lungs, the air going down to the very
roots of the world. Something stirs in the
tangled undergrowth of this
new day, something silver
darts around the
corner of wakening,
shattering the dream-mirror.

Suddenly there is light and
oxygen, and the heart picks up its
heavy load and
walks.

Sipping vodka

I speed over the Alps
and look brazenly down;
I glide over cathedrals
of ice. Flying buttresses
rise to meet me. Gargoyles
monkey about. Troglodyte
angels clank by.

Great ships

Great ships like trees in the
back yard, under the star
paths; navigators of the
night. From the top-mast of my
high window, I observe the
currents, and the
winds I know by their
smell. Tonight it's the
east wind, cold and
uneasy. Lost cats
crouch in the branches.
The yew berries have all
been trampled into the
ground. My husband is curled up
in his bunk – his shift is the early
morning. But I am the night watcher.
I call the stars to me and I
name them, each and every one, in
Arabic.

The healing touch

The barrier goes down. It glows red.
OTHER PEOPLE KEEP OUT, or you're dead.

But alone in the therapy room
I weave prayers on my ten-fingered loom.

The white-coated nurses have fled,
observe me through cameras instead.

They've tattooed a few dots on my skin
to show where the beams must go in.

I am raised on my altar of tin
Eli, lama sabachthani. Amen.

The machine hovers over my chest,
at a hair's breadth from me comes to rest.

It embraces me with a strange groan;
I don't budge while the healing goes on.

Now there's silence except for a bleep;
I half-open my eyes, take a peep.

The nurses creep in, realign
a body that's no longer mine.

They are gone before I can say 'Hi!'
Goodbye, Yaweh's angels, goodbye.

The barrier is down. It glows red.
PEOPLE KEEP OUT, or you're dead.

Moult

She kept the other breast. The hair
that had been fair grew back, black.

She found a crop of spuds under her arm.
They gouged them out and with curved needles

darned. Daisies lose their petals
in the scampering winds of May.

The dandelions' lush heads turn into clocks
and then they blow away.

But did you ever hear of 'eclipse plumage'?
Birds moult, you see. They must renew

their feathers every year because of wear
and tear. And wild fowl lose

flight feathers all at once. For six weeks
cannot fly. Some drakes turn into

pulsing sacs of dowdy brown and grey.
Camouflaged as water-hens,

they wedge themselves between the nest and nestlings,
reeds and sedge. Doomed for a season

to a slow decay – like her
(the one who lost the breast) and me

(oh prithee please do not enquire) – they wait
for nature's fledge.

The golden retriever grieves for her mate

The hooded crows roost early now,
November trees are black.
The sun goes down at 4 p.m.
and leaves a blood-stained track.

My antelope, my darling, my gazelle.

We calm her with valerian
and drops of chamomile,
infuse the roots of heliotrope
to soothe her for a while.

My antelope, my darling, my gazelle.

His last night was a rasping breath
that laboured up the stairs
and filled the house, and lodged behind
her sleepless eyes and ears.

My antelope, my darling, my gazelle.

She leans her head against our knees,
she follows us to bed
and lies stretched out upon the floor
as if she, too, were dead.

My antelope, my darling, my gazelle.

Thinking of Emily Dickinson

I could arrange, like her, to wear a snow-white flannel gown,
a violet posy at my throat, and in each hand a fresh-cut
heliotrope.

Six Irishmen could lift me up and bear me out the door,
around the garden, through the barn, across the fields of buzzing
buttercups.

If you insist, I'll listen to a passage from the Scriptures
and a prayer. But I must hear most needfully 'Last Lines'
in its entirety,

from Emily Brontë's pen. Then lower me into
eternity – the family plot. Engrave the words 'Called back'
on my small stone,

and on my death cert say my occupation was 'At home'.
I've left great bundles of rough poems with Maggie Maher, my maid.
She guards them

in her trunk. But I have ordered her, as literary
executor, to burn the junk. She'll carry out my wishes.
She's great at beds

and fires

and washing dishes.

The dowager queen's 'Te Deum'

And I have sworn before the king, my son,
who is a fool,
that I have never slept with Bishop Alwyn;
nor kissed
the Lord's anointed one, except at Michaelmas
his blessed ring.

King Edward, Sire, although you be my son,
you're but the pawn
of Robert de Jumièges. You give credence
to his tittle-tattle,
lies; ignore your mother's cries
of innocence.

Tomorrow, therefore, I will walk through flame
and clear my name
in Winchester Cathedral. And you,
my sovereign liege,
if God is just, you'll be dishonoured, lose
the people's trust,

receive a thousand lashes of the cane.
Tonight
with Spanish lace upon my head, I keep a vigil
at St. Swithin's
tomb. Adumbral centaurs recognize
my pain,

and stone-faced angels hanging in the vault;
and looming griffins,
basilisks with fatal breath; and dragons;
nameless winged
and taloned things that lurk between the cloister
and the slype.

I call to witness husbands, wives, and knights
caparisoned;
and black-swathed nuns, and maidens, merry widows,
tonsured monks,
recumbent figures stretched out on a slab,
that I am not

at fault. Cyclamens grow wild
beyond the walls,
the towering lime-trees drip. Winter waters
gather
in the crypt. The wyvern slythes. At dawn
the whole of England

comes to stare when I take off my shoes,
strip to my shift.
I call upon the God who saved Susanna,
and cross the burning
ploughshares in bare feet. I must admit
that, much to my

surprise, I walk on air. I swoon, I think,
I blaze with light.
I'm onyx, topaz, beryl, jasper, chrisolyte.
Edward, the King,
my son, who is a fool, shits on his throne
beside the altar

rail. His great men wring bejewelled hands,
grow pale.
Robert de Jumièges sets sail for France.

Perceval's sister

Who has the loveliest hair in the world?
Whisper, whisper, Perceval's sister.

Who turns it into a belt for a sword?
Ho, hum, said Perceval's sister,
Pellinore's daughter, the holy nun.

Who leads the knights on the path of the Grail?
Whisper, whisper, Perceval's sister.

With eyes like a cat's to light up the trail?
Ho, hum, said Perceval's sister,
Pellinore's daughter, the holy nun.

Who offers her veins to the sharp little knife?
Whisper, whisper, Perceval's sister.

Who fills a bowl with the rose of her life?
Ho, hum, said Perceval's sister,
Pellinore's daughter, the holy nun.

Who came in a ship with sails of milk?
Whisper, whisper, Perceval's sister.

And left in a barge all hung with black silk?
Ho, hum, said Perceval's sister,
Pellinore's daughter, the holy nun.

Who will wait in the ground till it's time to be wed?
Whisper, whisper, Perceval's sister.

Will the hair she cut off grow back on her head?
Ho, hum, said Perceval's sister,
Pellinore's daughter, the holy nun.

Long-distance Swimmer

Hungry for water she lowers herself
into lakes.
She stares at her face in the mere.

Bare but for Speedos and membrane-like cap,
she divines
where to go by a trembling of hands,

follows a ley-line through bog-hole and quarry
and dam.
She hangs Holy Marys on bushes,

she wades through the slobs, descends the dank steps
to the well.
Cheered on by St. Gobnait and nine grazing

deer, a badger, an otter, a fox and a
hare,
she dives into rivers, she butterflies

over the weir. She crawls up canals.
Rises and
falls at the lock. When the keeper has

opened the gates with his hydraulic key,
she shakes herself
loose of her togs and her cap.

Her neck disappears. She turns grey. Grows a fur coat
and claws.
Her limbs fuse in a silvery flash

as she swims for dear life out to sea.

November visit

Some go round naked, in the Hallowe'en masks
of their faces.
Some are strapped into giant perambulators.

Ownerless dentures are moaning on bath chairs.
Vacant skulls
gape at the moon. Kitty

is curled on her cushion; the stump of her lost tail
well-bearded
with fur. Tommy is widdling;

his little-boy penis hangs down like a piece
of wet string.
Under his trousers, Father

is wearing a nappy; he stores a zoo-language
deep
in his throat. It's tablets, like Smarties,

for beddy-byes now, and nursie's hand cold
on his brow.
Father peeps through the rails of his cot

at the star-cracker night. The Great Bear, as always,
is prowling
about. The hungry fox waits

at the gate. Orion is pulling the sword
from his belt.
It's too late to go zimmering out.

Strangers come shimmering in through the wall,
move their mouths,
wet the flop of his cheek. Father purses

his lips, blows out words one by one. Like bubbles
they pop
in the air till the strangers go blank,

disappear. 'What to do? What to do?' He dials
nine-nine-nine
on the palm of his hand. He presses

a fist to his ear; hears the Angel of God
on the line.
Outside, the apples

ferment on the trees. Father puts down the phone.
He rests
his great head on his knees.

Prince Lucifer

Prince Lucifer, the great God's darling son; the favourite,
    the loyal one;
the chief of all the angels; the one who wore the sapphired
    crown; the one whose eyes
were bright and dark, the sunset and the morning star;
    the one whose locks lit up
the Northern sky.

Lucifer. Light-bearer. The names of stars his litanies and
    attributes.
A galaxy of light the wonder-hair that sparked and
    glowed, that kindled fires
in icy waste, in frozen steppe. Thus Lucifer the prince
    before his fall.
But when he fell,

when he uprose against his sovereign Liege, the god who
    made him, Abba, Father,
Daddy: when Lucifer the prince, betrayed his Father's trust,
he fell from zenith platform, from the heights, from far
    above the sky we see,
and all the earth

went mad awhile, and all the lights went out.

Saint Catherine

After the miracle,
glued to the spot,
an icon in gold-leaf and scarlet,

she strokes the spiked wheel
as she would a pet dog.
The Emperor gapes;
gifts her a necklace, a necklace

of blood. Milk flows
from the miracle head
as it rolls off the block.
Bright as a nimbus it hangs

on the air, bearing
a crown. A crucifix
sprouts in the clasp
of her hands; black as the clay

that sticks to her feet,
beckoning once,
before sucking her in.

Hocus-pocus

Magician by day, he fools her with his hocus-pocus.
Pulls doves from his sleeves, jack-rabbits, Great Danes. A touch
of his wand and a baby grows under her smock.

By night a mere man with a cone on his head, he loses
his nerve at the thought of her belly ballooning with child.
He plies her with gin and hot baths; makes her jump

from the top of the stairs. The baby seeps out, disappears
in the sheets. He weeps as mosquitoes whine over the feast.
Strange lizards dart up the walls, slide over

her blood-splattered thighs. He fetches infusions of hyssop
and moistens her lips with a sponge. Turns away to throw up.
He waves his wand – useless at night – dons his star-studded

cape; throws flames from his uvula; thrusts a bright sword
down his throat. Hocus-pocus. The clotted suns rise in a bubble.
Behind the black breast of the chimney, the crickets *cri-cri*.

The crossing

The little boy was feather light, his countenance
amazing bright. I sat him on my shoulder.

He quivered with anticipation of delight
and half of fright as I stepped in the water.

The sky grew dark. The wind whipped up the corners
of my cloak. I leaned upon my staff of knotted

oak. The river rose. It ran full spate. But
as I lunged towards the farther shore,

my spine began to bend and break beneath the toddler's
sudden monstrous weight. I stumbled, pitched

the child into the foam. He, like a millstone,
sank. The whole world shook. I groped for him

with blinded hands, but barely made it back to land,
alone. My gilly-dog, a hound with web-like

paws, and eyes illumed, plunged in
from the high bank. Sucked down by some strange undertow,

he found the leaden child and pulled him out.
I gave the boy the kiss of life, and he was wondrous

haloed all about. 'You cheeky brat',
I cried, 'What were you at? We could have drowned

all three.' 'Forgive me, sir, I made you bear
the sorrows of mankind across the flood,

as well as me.' My gilly-dog bowed low
before his lord. I barely bent my knee

till I looked up and saw the child
nailed to a bloody tree.

About the Author

Dorothy Molloy was born in Ballina, Co. Mayo in 1942. She studied languages at University College Dublin, after which she went to live in Madrid and Barcelona. During her time in Spain, she worked as a researcher, as a journalist and as an arts administrator. She also had considerable success as a painter, winning several prizes and exhibiting widely. After her return to Ireland in 1979, she continued painting but also began writing poetry.

Her first collection, *Hare Soup*, was accepted by Faber and Faber, but Dorothy contracted cancer and died ten days before its publication. The papers she left after her death contained enough unpublished poems for two further books, which have been assembled by her husband, Andrew Carpenter. The first of these posthumous collections, *Gethsemane Day*, was published by Faber and Faber in 2007. This volume, *Long-distance Swimmer*, is the final collection of her work.